HOW TO BEAT

MICROSOFT'S

Minesweeper
Advanced

By

Mike Riley

This book was written as I sailed across the South Pacific from Bora Bora to Tonga.

I wrote a few pages and then rushed up on deck every ten minutes to make sure we weren't about to be sunk by some monster wave or super tanker.

Good thing we weren't, huh?

Table of Contents

Introduction

Minesweeper is a revolution that has refused to die. It was invented in the early years of Microsoft up in Redmond, Washington. The need then, was to hire people with bright minds, who could build the Microsoft empire into the incredible success it became in next few years after the release of 3.0.

The problem was how to pick the right people. Gates and Allen didn't care if prospective employees had a background in developing operating systems. Very few people did in those far ago days. They didn't care if they were college graduates. Gates quit Yale in his junior year. Instead they searched for the best minds available. But how? Sometimes college graduates were fine in you wanted stock answers; inventive, imaginative minds were a resource very hard to corral.

After a few false steps, they developed the first of many versions of Minesweeper as a tool for eliminating the hordes of job applicants hounding Microsoft in those days of incredible growth in the dawn of personal computers.

Gates and Allen wanted a selection process that would separate applicants who possessed pure intelligence and inventiveness from those who either lacked a high level of intelligence or who had never learned to use what they were born with. It succeeded beautifully.

Not only could the ability to beat Minesweeper indicate a superior mind (Note the Pun. They were sweeping the job applicant pool for good minds!) but it also indicated a mind capable of inventive thinking.

It didn't take long for future applicants to realize that if they wanted in, they better bone up on beating Minesweeper, then released, bundled with Microsoft 3.0. Soon prospective job applicants were playing Minesweeper at work, in bars, on the bus, at the dinner table and before going to bed. Soon others, not interested in Microsoft joined in on the Minesweeper craze. It became a very popular game.

It took awhile for anyone to realize that playing minesweeper was improving the player's attention span, the time that a player could keep his brain turned 'on'; the length of time that a person could eliminate other thoughts from her or his brain and concentrate on just one task. This was a breakthrough. At first it was thought that practice was allowing players to 'cheat' by improving performance. Soon however, Microsoft realized that they were tapping an unusual resource of the populace- adaptable minds.

Universities had been trying to train minds for centuries and for the most part failing miserably. The few who managed to totter and stagger their way through the prerequisite and repetitive first two years of college life, and still keep their initial enthusiasm and joy for learning, were few indeed. Most of the graduates would have been better served with a classical education of the Great Works learned while sitting under a tree. Because the University experience punished mistakes, it also eliminated the desire to experiment, to try new things.

Microsoft didn't have time for sitting under trees or for coddling students through 4 years of baby sitting either. There had to be a better way.

The better way came bundled with XP with three versions of Minesweeper. Beginner, Intermediate and Advanced. Beginner was the Minesweeper from old, the one almost everyone had become good at. Intermediate was for more practice. Advanced, where there were 99 mines spread over a 480 square grid was for training and for job placement. For a new player, it took well over three minutes to solve the advanced puzzle. Three minutes of intense, brain squeezing thought. It was thought that anyone who could keep their brain turned 'on' and concentrating on one problem for three minutes was worth looking at. He or she might be capable of much more.

It is an urban myth that with the release of XP, Advanced Minesweeper carried a hidden program that contacted Microsoft if a player ever beat Minesweeper Advanced with a time of 100 seconds or better. If and when the magic number was reached, the program contacted Microsoft the next time the computer was connected to the internet and Microsoft then contacted the player with an invitation for a job interview. I have tried many times to contact Microsoft seeking the truth of this myth. The only answer was, "We neither confirm nor deny any thing to do with Minesweeper."

Microsoft attempted to correlate IQ with Minesweeper success and with job performance. IQ, Intelligence Quotient, a number derived from the ability to perform certain tasks learned in school or thought to be related to school success, seemed to have little correlation with job performance success. Minesweeper Advance success, however, has an amazing correlation with success in the work force in a job where fast thinking and intuitive thought were required.

In the new millennium, resentment grew over Microsoft's desire to continue bundling the original structure of Minesweeper released with XP. Users became disillusioned by the game's first move which often resulted in blowing up. Users wanted to be given a free pass. They wanted to always end up hitting an open square when starting the game.

Microsoft resented this. They felt that the human brain did have extra sensory abilities and that one of those was the ability to sense the very near future. (In Microsoft's defense, these days Police Forces worldwide use people, thought to have ESP, to find missing persons, especially children, with remarkable success.) Supposedly (Again an urban myth, lets keep those lawyers in Redmond!) Microsoft's hidden program measured the number of Advanced games played where the player picked a non mine square. When that number reached 99 in a row, that also sent a message to Microsoft that often resulted in a job offer. However, starting in Microsoft Vista, your first click always lands on a non mine square. Bummer, huh? (Actually, since I almost always hit a mine in those old days, I am just as glad to get on with it. Still I always hoped that I could have some ESP. You know, be one of those mutants with weird and wonderful powers, or at least have some idea of what my wife is talking about when she wakes me from a deep sleep! But alas, I seem to be boringly normal. Well, normal with a slightly faster mind, which is why I am writing this book!)

So, do you want to join the 'in' crowd? Do you want to develop your brain into a powerful tool to solve difficult puzzles and questions. Do you want to be able to turn your brain on, on command? Do you want to be able to think a half a second ahead of everyone else? To be able to answer the question first? To tell a joke faster? To get the pun quicker? You can. The tool to train your brain is right there on your computer. Go for it. Heck, you could always frame that invite from Microsoft and hang it on you den's wall! Imagine inviting you pals over and showing off! The thrill of it! For you girls, guys minds are slightly demented, they were made that way. Let a sexy girl walk by and every man in sight instantly forgets the problem he was working on and stares at the girl, perhaps with his mouth sagging open. Its just the way men are made. Girls brains are clearly superior, however, beware. At times, men can think with astounding quickness, usually when girls aren't around!

Are you ready to beat Minesweeper Advanced? This book is not concerned with Minesweeper Beginner or Intermediate. It is assumed that the reader has already mastered such skills. If he or she hasn't, they will have no trouble doing so after studying the next chapter.

The Easy Give Me's

Minesweeper is all about patterns. If you can recognize some often reoccurring patterns, winning the game will become much easier. No, this is not a cheat. Intelligence is based on spotting and recognizing patterns in a task, and reacting appropriately. It is how the CIA operates. (Wait, maybe that isn't saying much!)

The yellow light between a green and red on a traffic signal is a pattern. Our minds don't say, "Oh, a yellow light, a red light will be next. I better start stopping." The brain sees the pattern and without thought, tells the muscles to react. Patterns are a very necessary part of life. A pygmy in the jungle hears the birds suddenly fall quiet and he instantly, without thought, jumps for the nearest tree and climbs up madly, sure that a predator in the area and may be after him.

Some of these patterns in Minesweeper are so easy to spot and reoccur so often I call them a 'Give Me' after a short putt in golf that your opposing player calls out, 'That's a give me,' and knocks your ball back to you, reliving you of having to make the putt. (This is supposed to 'knock' you off your game as success breeds success, freebies breed laziness and failure.) In Minesweeper, the easy patterns are a great place to start and are a building block for more complicated patterns to follow. Don't ignore them thinking they are too easy. They won't knock you off your game. Rather they are necessary to understand more difficult techniques to come.

Here is a common first look at the beginning of a random game. There are a lot of Give Me's here. Let's look at one of them.

Anytime there is an exposed 4, a bell should ring in your head. In this case the 1 in the upper right is a given, a mine, and the 4 then has no other choice but to claim all the squares about it, not eliminated by the 1. There is another exposed 4. Can you see it? Think and then read on.

The 4 above the 2 in the previous screen is a give me. It has no choice but to claim the left squares as mines. Can you work it out? Don't go past this screen until you can. Think about each square. Be like Spock. Logic is the purpose of life.

(See if you can make Spock's 'Live long and Prosper' hand sign!

Sorry, I always wanted to be an astronaut but turned into a sailor instead. Bummer, huh?)

Each 'Give Me' will build upon the previous one. Be sure you understand each advancement. Minesweeper develops the ability to be insightful. Insightfulness can best be defined as the ability to reach a correct decision with insufficient information. A very useful trait in our and any other civilization.

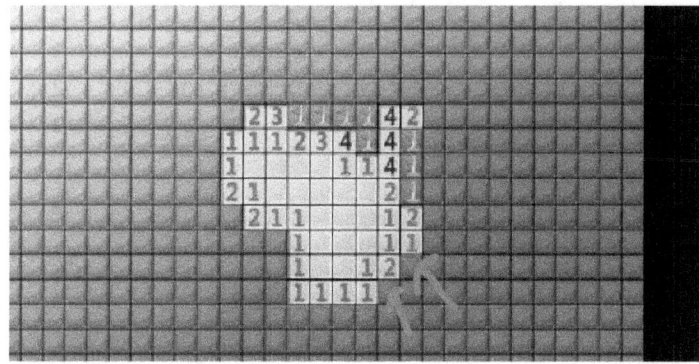

On the bottom right of the board under the 4's are two 1's and with a two between them. This Give Me is very common in Minesweeper. I am sure you can figure it out.

This opening of the game was caused by choosing the two 1's as mines and then clicking all the adjacent 1's as non mines. This really opened up the game didn't it? (Warning. Opening the game is not always a successful strategy. More on this later.) Look now at the two 2's in a row to the right of our first pair of 2's and to the

left lower area from the same pair. These are definitely 'Give Me's'. I know that you can spot these and know what to do.

We didn't open much adjacent territory this time. But we did expose some other Give Me's. Look at the lower left. See the 4 surrounded by 2's and mines? We don't know which of the two squares will be a mine. We do know that it will be either the four or the 2 to the double 2's left. Only one of them can be a mine. Think about that for a minute. No matter which one is a mine, the 1, third in line, the square next to the 2 is not a mine. This Give Me is a little trickier. Don't leave this page until you are sure that you understand why the 1 can not be a mine. The pair of 1's down and right of the original pair of 2's is a Give Me. I am sure you can spot them.

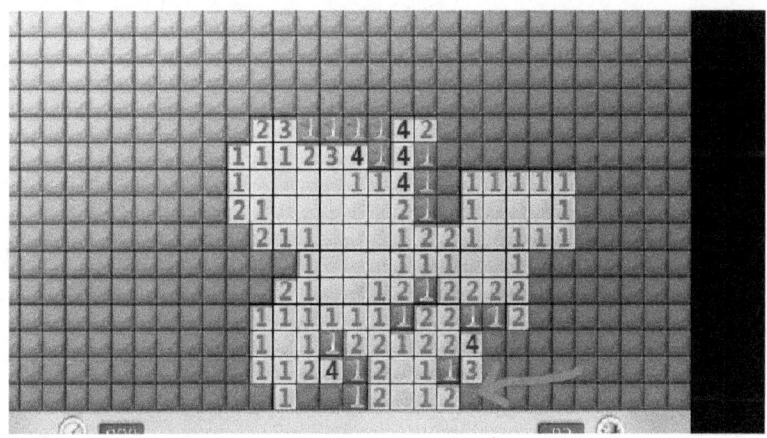

This is very clear I think. No surprises here. Can you see the Give Me on the right bottom? You know that the two is going to be a mine and of the 4 and 3 above, only one can be a mine.

We have gone as far as we can using these numbers and Give Me's. Later in the book we will learn more advanced methods to proceed from this location. But for now let's move else where on the board and look for more Give Me's. How about all those exposed 1's everywhere on the board. Let's click them all and see what we have. I count six. How many do you see?

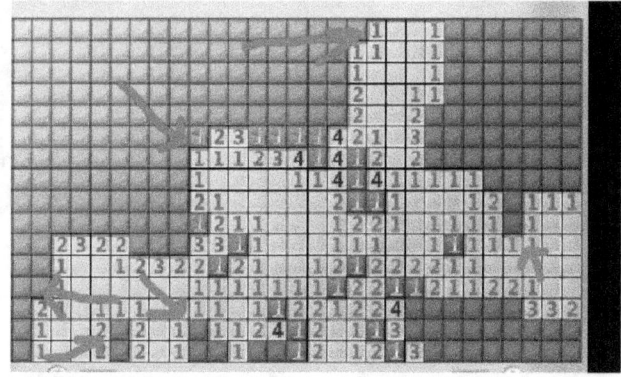

Amazing what clicking a few 1's will accomplish! Now look what we have. Give Me's everywhere! How many of the Give Me's that we have already studied can you spot? I see thirteen. Can you spot any more? Let's see what happens when we click all the Give Me's we can find.

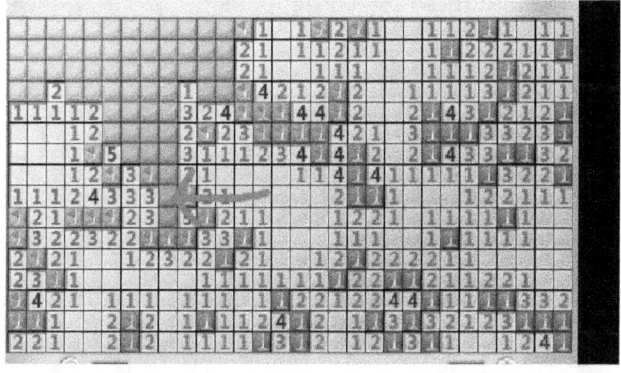

Wow! Given that a lot of Give Me's were exposed while playing the original Give Me's, it is still an astounding clearing of the board. Unfortunately there is only one Give Me exposed now, but it is one we haven't explored yet. Oh, lucky day! Look on the left middle of the board. There are two vertical 3's bottomed out with by a 232 combo, of which only two are in play. The bottom 3 already has two of its required three mines used up. However, the top 3 has only one 3 used up. That means of the two uncovered squares to the left of the two vertical 3's, only one can be a mine.

That in turn means that the square above the second 3 has to be a mine. Let's see what happens.

Wait. Do you understand that? The two bottom mines need one more to feed either one of the above 3's. But only one of the tow vertical 3's can be a mine. That means that the third vertical cloaked square (probably a Romulan!) has to be a mine! Right? Sometimes an insight takes time. Study it. Study helps.

That really opened it up and exposed some other new Give Me's. Look at the 5 in the middle left of where we were just working. Count the squares around it. Three. All of them have to be mines. Now look at the 1 just above of the 3 to the right and above of the 5 we were just working with. The 3 says that one of the twos on either side of the 3 has to be a mine. That means that the three spaces above the 1 cannot be mines. Can you figure it all out. If you were really playing those moves and continue what you have already learned and this is what happens.

VICTORY!

Wasn't that easy! Oh, you want the intervening steps? You know them all. They were all Give Me's. Sometimes that is all you need to win, but not often. Before we go on to more difficult concepts, lets do a few more Give Me's. You know, just to build up your confidence! Nah! This is easy! Right?

The brain resists insights. Part of the brain, thinks remembering is all important. It doesn't want to think, it wants to remember. A smaller part of the brain likes to think. To calculate. To work out which poker hand will win without seeing all the cards. To decide what size beams have to be to keep the roof from falling in. You have to encourage this part of the brain to work, to figure. Otherwise it will just sit there and vegetate. Minesweeper, like crossword puzzles, is good for brain health.

Take a look at the two 1's below. This happens a lot in Minesweeper. This is a really automatic Give Me. It doesn't matter what number might lie below the two 1's, it is not a mine. Absolutely never. Really!

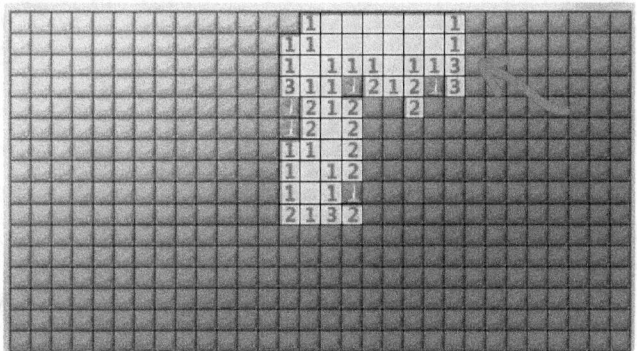

There is an oriental belief that a man of true knowledge acts without thinking. Sounds stupid, doesn't it? In the case of Minesweeper, it is true. Give Me's like the one above happen so often that thinking about it just slows down your game times and makes you spend your thinking time on areas where it is not needed. Learn not to think about a Give Me like the one above. Just react. Act without thinking. Thinking is not necessary if you totally know the answer. I know it goes against everything you were taught in college. Welcome to the real world. The world beyond school. Sometimes, you don't need to think. Thinking is counter productive. Stop thinking. React.

The same is true in real life. Some things are give me's. You already know the scenario. Thinking about and railing against the idiocy of it just slows you down. Treat such events like Minesweeper give me's. If you know it, don't think. Just do the required actions and save your brain power for more interesting problems. Are we uselessly adding stress to our life, thinking about things that should be a Give Me?

Maybe those oriental guy weren't so stupid after all? Enough philosophy. Back to beating Minesweeper. Let's complete the two areas we just discussed.

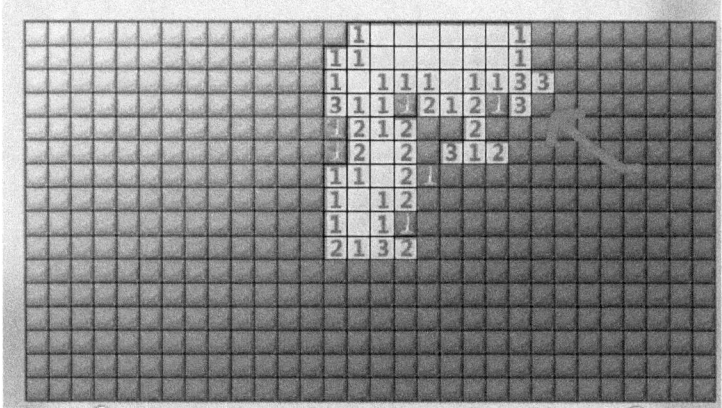

Wow! Now we are talking. This game is really opening up. See anymore Give Me's?

How about the 3 with two spaces next to it? There is no question here. The spaces around the 3 must be mines. There are so many Give Me's on this screen! Are you ready to find some mines?

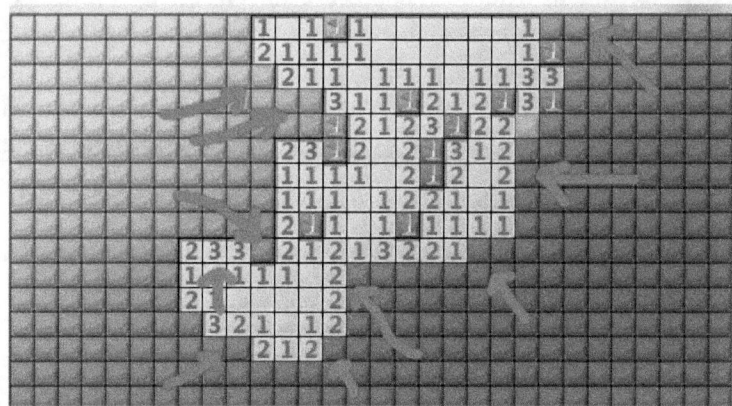

There are a lot of Give Me's. Can you see what each arrow is indicating? I had a calculus teacher once who was asked how many days of class, students could miss without being penalized. The teacher replied, "Well, none. Not even a minute. If you miss one minute, one insight, you will never catch up. You will have given yourself a penalty." It is much the same here. Don't leave this page till you have understood why all those arrows are there. Here is the next page. Ready?

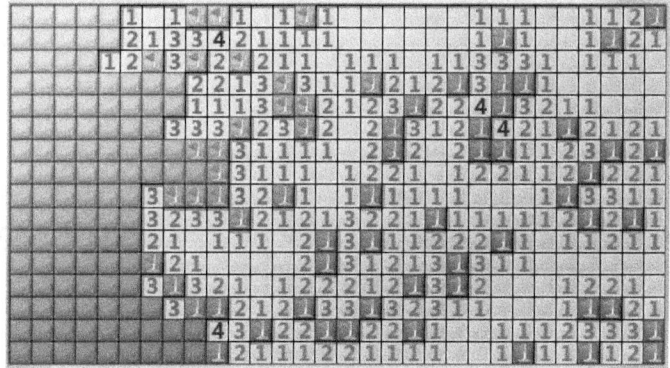

OK. Now we are in trouble. There are no Give Me's left. Gulp! Let's try some harder games. Like this one! Actually, they aren't that much harder. What is harder is the conception of the move and retaining the memory of it to use later. Just like Give Me's they are logical. We will return to this game and complete it then.

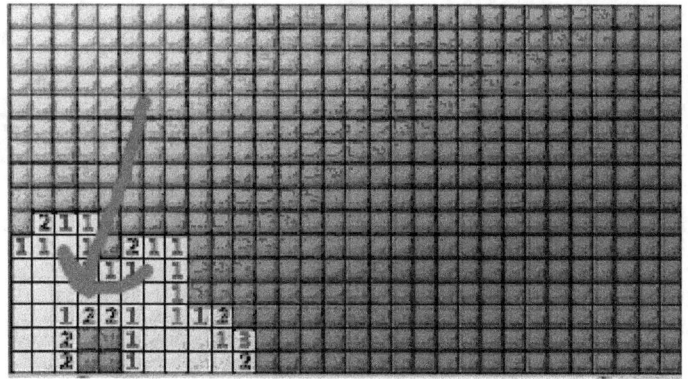

Wait. Before we do, lets continue to explore more Easy Give Me's. See, I am not heartless no matter what my wife might say! For example, if two 2's were up against the edge of the board, both of them would have to be mines as seen below.

In this case both 2's on the left are mines, both 2's on the top are mines and the bottom square on the right is not one. Got that? Equally well, the 2,3 combo on the lower right are both mines, the 1 above satisfies the 3's demand for mines.

Look below at all the 1212121 combos. Any time you spot an open 2 surrounded by 1's, the 2 is always not a bomb. Always.

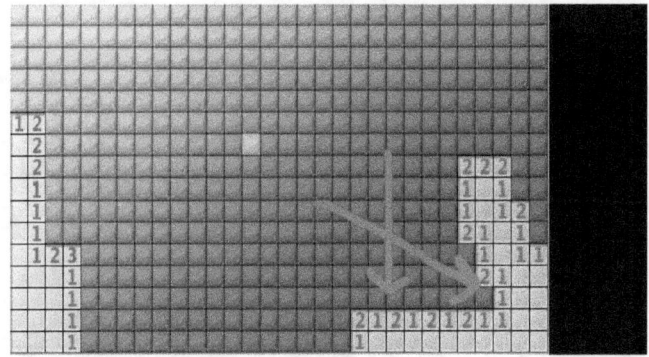

The proof is in the pudding. (What? I always looked for proofs in my text books. No wonder I had trouble with advanced calculus!) Sorry. (Taurus's always tell bad jokes) The proof is below.

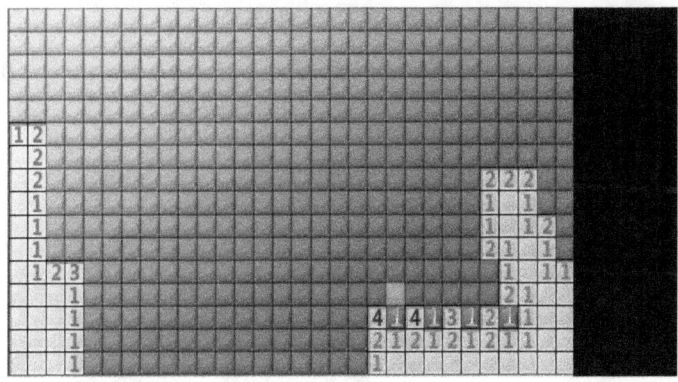

If you tried to work this out each and every time, it would drive you crazy. Accept this pattern and play it without thinking.

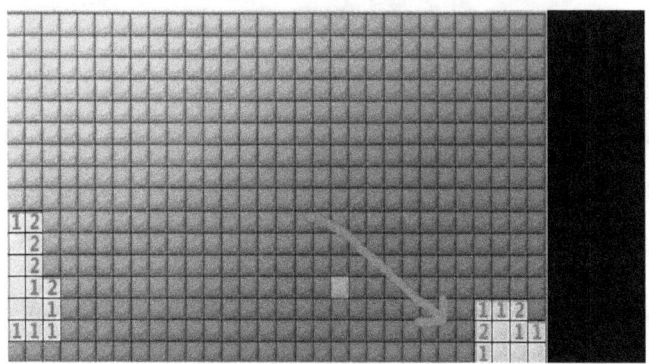

Whenever a 121 sequence is next to the edge of the board, the two, like above, is a space and the two 1's are mines. Always.

The next example is a little trickier. Not that it is hard. The boxes below the 2 and 4 are obviously mines. One of the boxes across from the 1 and 4 are mines. That means that the box indicated by the arrow must be a mine.

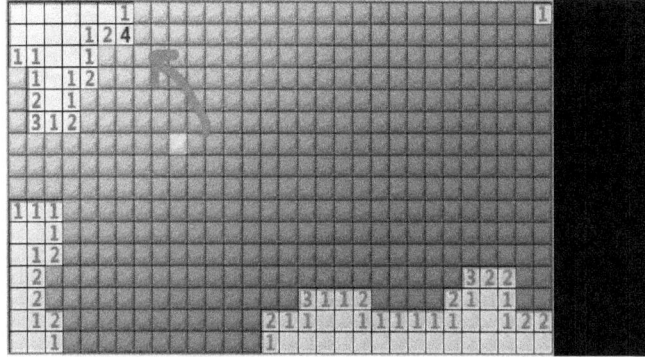

Thusly. Note that I had to solve more of the puzzle to get back to the box in question.

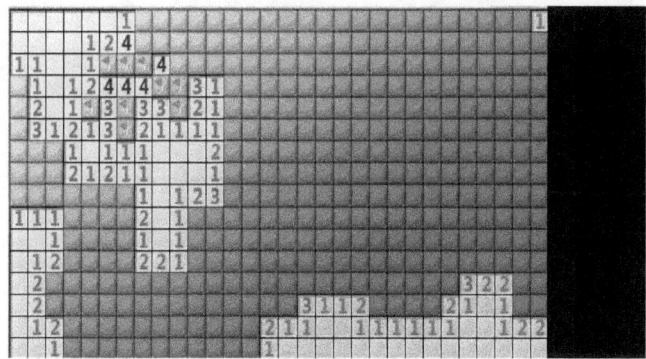

Here is an easier example, next. Note the 122 sequence. Every time you see this you know that the second two as indicated is a mine. Every time. Trust your patterns, Luke.

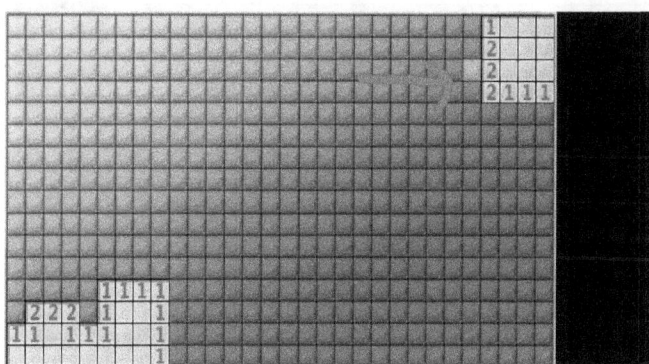

To prove this I had to solve for the entire game starting at the bottom left. This really is not difficult to do, once in awhile.

Here is another basic Give Me. The 22 against the edge you already know. The 232, below is obvious with a bit of thought.

Some games are really difficult. Very. But you can happen on to an easy game once in a while. I guessimate that there are 3 very difficult, 6 kind of difficult to every easy game. If you follow the guides in this book, the easy one you can beat while talking to your friends, you will be able beat all of the 'kind of difficult games' if you can keep your brain going and you will be able to beat the very difficult ones if you are a good guesser. Guessing is and important part of Minesweeper. More on this later on. Here is the resolved game below from above.

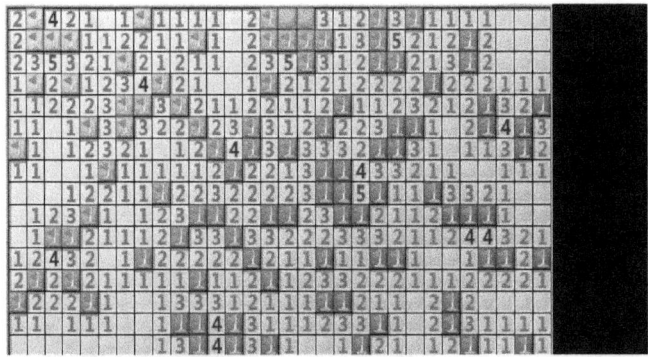

But before we go into what is best called 'Tricky Ones.' Let's look at the fact that sometimes Minesweeper will open up vast areas of the board with a single click and at other times, you have to struggle and fight for every space. We have all experienced it. We have all cursed at it. We just saw it happen in the game above. How can we control it?

Opening Up The Game

Minesweeper was designed to award insightfulness. Microsoft wanted to select people who could see behind corners without peeking. Some people can. They do it by recognizing patterns and then go one step farther. They do it by observing the patterns and seeing a pattern beyond the patterns. Seeing a pattern among the patterns.

This is not some heebie-jeebie, ESP, weird science fiction, elitist bull sh_t. It is something that regular people do everyday and don't even realize it. When you are driving along, approaching an intersection and observe the cross traffic on the left slowing for some unknown reason, little alarms go off in your head and immediately you start slowing suspecting something different is happening out of sight to the right without thinking! Maybe it is a crash, maybe it is a drunk driver, maybe it is some kids speeding, maybe it is a cop on the prowl giving end of the month tickets, the thing is we don't know what it is but still we react to it. We all do this. It is because we spend large amounts of our life driving and have been trained to realize that driving is a dangerous and potentially lethal endeavor.

It is the same with Minesweeper except often we do realize what the pattern is, as there are a finite number of possible patterns in the game, unlike in real life.

If you can see beyond the corner and react to it, people call it insightfulness. Microsoft calls it a marketable commodity and rewards it. They reward it in Minesweeper by opening up the game with one click of the mouse.

Here is the trick, the game only opens up with an insightful move. It has to be a bit of insightfulness that Minesweeper thinks is advanced. Sometimes I do a bit of clicking that I think was really, really advanced and Minesweeper totally ignores me. Bummer!
Other times, the gates of Heaven open and the whole game is displayed on my little screen. Why Minesweeper rewards some insight and not others is a good question, unless they are just mimicking life's capriciousness. Either way, you can't beat Minesweeper with decent times without insightfulness. If you haven't already, it is time to practice. Soon, your husband/wife will wonder why you have turned into a super spouse anticipating their every wish!

In the pages ahead we will show examples of this and hopefully guide you on your way to seeing life in a different way. This was and is Microsoft's aim. To change, to alter the way people, the way employees think. (Sorry, lawyers might be reading this, Microsoft's alleged aim!)

To discover people who when asked what 3x3x3 is, respond 3^3. To find people who when asked which is better apples or oranges, reply, "Yes." To discover and train people who can determine that it was the butler in the library with the candlestick a few seconds faster than everyone else and with one less clue card. (They watch the patterns the other players are following.)

Success at Minesweeper is determined by the ability to turn your brain on to high power, voluntarily. Minesweeper trains you to keep your brain turned on to high power for longer and longer times. As fast as your brain is now, it can be trained to work as fast as a crystal laser. (No one thinks as fast as a plasma laser!)

Think fast, think creatively, think beyond the corner, think with insight. If Adolf Hitler had been a Minesweeper fan, he never would have invaded Russia and stayed in the winter. Retreat, allow the silly Russians to rebuild with their limited supplies, invade again in the spring. (Actually, historically, make peace, withdraw, reinvade, over and over until the Russians give up. This is what the Americans tried in Vietnam; the problem was, politically, they were not allowed to make peace. Bummer, huh?

Don't Open That Game!

It is sad but true. The world is not on your side. If fact, half the time they might even be out to get you! Just because you are paranoid, doesn't mean you can't be an asset to civilization. In Minesweeper, tricky pro-noids (opposite of paranoid!) are, every time you solve a bit of the puzzle, quick as a wink, the game solves a little bit of the puzzle else where on the board where you aren't looking! Wonderful, you say? Terrible, say I. (Sorry, I really loved Treasure Island as a boy.)

The problem is that they clear the easy spots and leave hard areas that could have been easily solved if we had the chance. Minesweeper released with XP was decent in that you could double right click and turn off the game opening tendency. However, with the release of Vista, (when Microsoft was practically forced to open the game on the first click) this right click move was deleted from the game.

Now there is no hope except before clicking such an easy move, a move that is such a give-me it is unbelievable, check out the other moves in the game. Often Minesweeper, reorganizes your game, taking away the easy moves, leaving cloaked squares that normally would have opened, leaving instead rough, tough, practically unsolvable moves. A little fore sight will prevent this from happening.

Perhaps the most difficult thing in life is to me diving on a coral reef, see a lobster and sticking my hand in his hole to pull him out and to find as so often happens, there is a moray eel living in the same hole and he considers your hand an unpardonable invasion. He bites your finger and holds on. You now have three choices. Pull your finger out in fear and in an understandable reaction. This will strip your finger of any meat (read finger muscle) which if you are really lucky will lead to amputation of the finger. Worse case scenario is amputation of the entire hand. Two. Hold your hand still until, hopefully, the moray grows tired of such a disgusting piece of meat in his mouth. (Remember he likes fish!) Hopefully he will let go before you drown! Or, three, force your finger deep into his throat, causing him to gag and to open his mouth wide to get rid of this annoying, disgusting thing in his mouth.

Sorry for the trip on the wild side. Not reacting to a suddenly open game is much the same. Don't react suddenly. Study the game. Memorize it as best you can. As quick as you can. Then click. You will win many more games.

OK. This only happens once in ten games, irregardless, once you are a devotee of the game, such distinguishing attributives are the soul of the game. Be aware. Watch out for trickiness. Minesweeper is not on your side. You will have to out-wit, out play, out last the game if you will allow me to steal from TV (the horror) programs!

However without such trickiness, it will be very difficult to win in less that 101 seconds.

The Mouse

Unless you are a dedicated game player, your mouse might be old and slow. You cannot beat Minesweeper Advanced in a decent time with a creaky old mouse. In fact, using an old and slow mouse is an exercise in frustration. Don't do it. Life is too short.

I am not going to sit here and tell you which mouse to use other than it has to be an optical mouse. I hope you are not still using a trackball mouse. If you are, stop. You aren't still using a slide rule are you?

Everyone has their favorite mouse. You want the one that fits perfectly into your hand, that moves perfectly without the slightest effort. You should just think, and the mouse will move, almost like magic. You will discover that you can be determining the configuration in one part of the Minesweeper board and have your mouse clearing the board on another part without looking at the mouse location, routinely. You can't do that without a mouse that matches you perfectly.

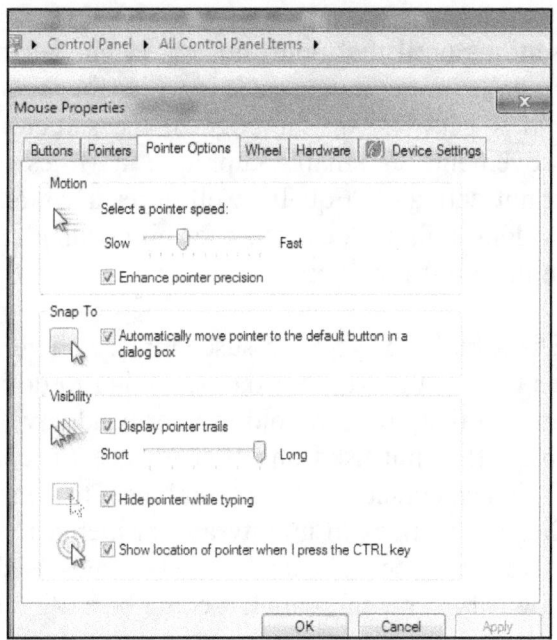

Along with the mouse is the mouse pad. Everyone prefers different ones. The mouse can't react well with a less than brilliant mouse pad. Personally I like pulp magazines. They are free. New ones come every month. You can tear a page out every day and have a nice new mouse pad. If you get bored you can doodle on them without changing the performance of your mouse. But then I am widely known to be a ~~cheapo~~, economically insightful player!

Lastly the mouse can be adjusted to match your personality and hand speed by going to the Control Panel, Mouse, pointer options. Here are my settings.

The control button you might need to adjust is the pointer speed. A fact of life is the Minesweeper screen cannot be maximized (it can be enlarged by stretching the sides outwards with the curser.) and even if it could, it would be counter productive.

If the screen was not small enough to encompass in a glance, insightful play would be far more difficult. Being not maximizable (if that is a word), mouse movements have to be more precise.

Adjust your settings until the mouse matches your personality. I like to use long tails on the mouse as it is easier for me to find my mouse cursor if it gets lost on the edge of the screen. Because most mouse movements are small and precise in Minesweeper, the long tail does not activate. Equally well, after a while, a player gets so used to long tails it doesn't bother him or her. But by all means, disable the tail if it bothers you.

Carpal tunnel is a hassle if you are susceptible. There are many types of braces to ease the pain but the best thing to do is to get a wireless, 3D mouse that you can hold in your hand anywhere. No table is required. It is not used on a flat surface. It can be held upside down. You can click with you thumb next to your chest. A 3D mouse relies on changes in gravity and in inertia to move the curser on the screen. It does take a while to becomes used to it, but if you are worried about carpal tunnel, it could be a life changer.

It is my belief that the mouse buttons are not the cause of Carpal Tunnel syndrome. It is caused my spinning the mouse wheel. To make it easier on yourself, spin the wheel with your middle finger. (Tall Man)

Go to the store. Tell them you want to buy a mouse to play games with. They will understand. Buy a cheaper one of the selection they offer. (Minesweeper is not a game to them, it is a warm-up! The mouse they will want to sell to you is meant for very exotic games requiring incredible accuracy.) Oh, what the heck. Buy the best you can afford! You only live once!

Speed of Play

It is a mistake when you are beginning to play minesweeper to play too slow. The brain is at its best when it is challenged. Wait. Let me rephrase that. The kind of brain that Microsoft is looking for is at its best when it is challenged.

Often, when you are taking your time, trying not to make a mistake, checking everything twice, your brain loses that edge; it falls asleep. Don't get me wrong. It acts like it is alive and well and performing at its highest efficiency. But it isn't. It makes stupid mistakes.

Your mouse hits the square next to the one you intended to hit. You know that a square is a mine and yet you open it. These are actions of a bored brain, a brain begging you to find something interesting for it to do. Something that it can stick its teeth into. It wants to stop idling down the freeway. It wants to go as fast as it can. Let your brain go. Ask it to perform as fast as it can.

When you do amazing things happen. You stop making stupid mistakes. Your score drops, plummets, jumps off the waterfall. Your eyes start to shine with a gleam of passion, of achievement, of success.

With your Brain turned on, Minesweeper becomes addictive. Your brain likes to perform as fast as it can. It will want to do it more often. It will want to do it every day, all day.

Instead of sitting in front of the computer all day long, do what Microsoft intended so many years ago. Use the skills you have and will learn playing Minesweeper and use them in real life. Know what your boss wants before he thinks of it. Anticipate what your enemies will try next and be ready with a counter move before they open their eyes in the morning. Life will become far more interesting!

Tricky Ones

The Give Me's are fairly obvious. Oh, stop worrying. Tricky Ones aren't that tough. Stop being a worrywart. They are a little bit harder, just a bit. A little bit. Let's try a couple.

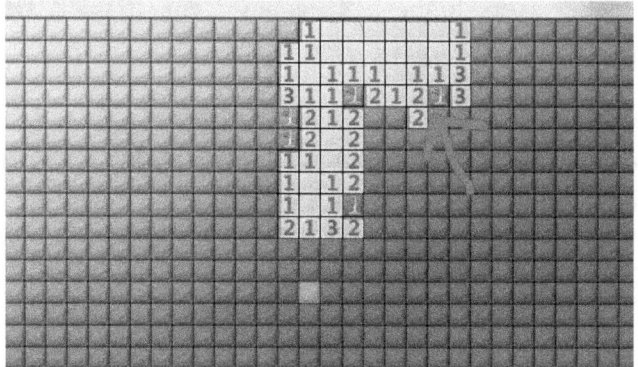

Take a look at the two vertical 2's indicated. The top 2 shown needs a second mine. It has to be one of the two immediately below it, but we don't know which one. However, since one of those is a mine, the second 2 already has its required two mines. That means all of the three spaces directly below cannot be mines.

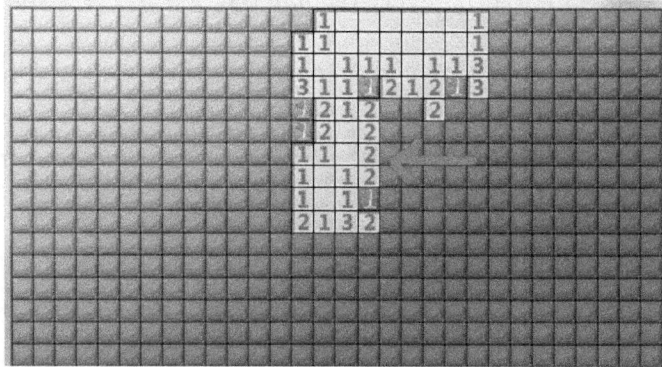

Take a look at the four vertical 2's indicated above. (I hope above. One is never sure what will happen to his treasured book once Kindle's computers have finished stretching it this way and that!)

Of the first two top 2's, only one can be a mine, which means that the third 2 must be a mine. If the third is a mine, that means that the fourth cannot be one. Can you figure all of that out? Take your time. It is going to become trickier as we go on, but I will go slower. Lets forget the above screen for a second and return to the game we left to rot a couple chapters ago. We ran out of Give Me's and got stuck. Lets see if we can figure it out now. Here is where we left it.

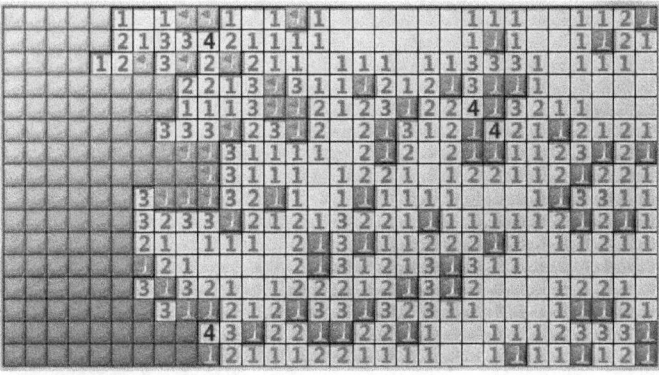

There are no Give Me's here. We have to use Tricky Ones! Whoa! Don't freak! Give me a break. You can do it!

The arrow indicates a mine with a 2 and a 3 above it. Of the 2 and the 3, only one can be a mine. Right? Do you see that? Stop and figure it out. Take your time.

Good. You got it. That means that the next 3 up has to be a mine. What? You can't figure it out? The trick is if both the 2 and 3 are bombs, the mine below will insist only one can be a mine. Right? Really. Work it out. Sorry, the going is harder now. But you can do it!

Here is an interesting screen. It looks like a game to be guessed at, however, with a little thought we can solve it.

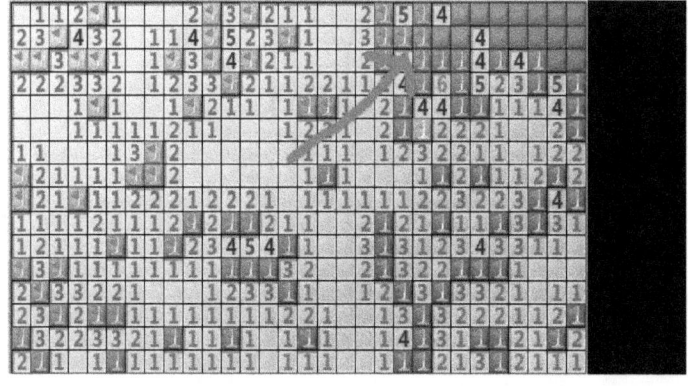

The topmost 4 indicated has two mines and three spaces around it. Two of those spaces must be mines. The next 4 over claims at least another mine. The 5 yet another. There are five mines yet to be found in the game. We have found 4 for sure. This is a good time to guess. In the next chapter we will get into guessing, or as Microsoft prefers to call it, solving a problem correctly with insufficient data. Guessing is a crucial part of the game, however, for now, we should proceed with logic, Mr. Spock like!

Here is a blow up of the problem. Don't be in a hurry. We are getting into the really nifty stuff now. The ways you can wow all the girls. Girls like guys who are smart. Who knows why? If they intend to spend their lives keeping men in the dark, why not a less than smart one? But they don't. Strange are the minds of women!

Lets click the top right square thinking it is a non-mine. That square is far away from the action. It seems safe. With any luck the game will think it is an insightful move and it will open the game up for us, making it an easy win, easy because we only have one lost mine. One as we kind of know where the other 4 are. Let's see what happens.

Warning! Warning! Warning! Wow! Watch out for this kind of thing! The game should have opened up. Maybe it didn't because Minesweeper is playing with our minds, but far more likely, our lost mine is somewhere in the surrounding squares next to that 1. That is good. We know more or less where it is.

That clarifies things. We can now click the leftmost square above the question marks with a fair degree of confidence.

That completes the game. It is plain sailing now. Yes? Think about it. Work it out in your mind. There is no clock clicking. Well, there is but we can ignore it. No one but ourselves are paying attention. You have all the time in the world, as long as the boss isn't wandering around, that is!

Here is an easier tricky one. Look at the 1 indicated and the 2 to the left of it. There is no way to know which of the two question marks is the mine. However, because of the 1, we know a lot about the area to the left.

Here I have used the 1 to open up the game a little. Now the two questions marks indicate a possible mine that the 3 needs. We don't know which one it is but we do know that the 1.2 combo to the left means that the further left 1 is not a mine.

We don't know which of the two question marks is a mine, the 4's third mine, but if you think about it, quickly, I hope, the 2 has to be a mine as the 1 to the 2's left is out of play.

This is the crux of beating Minesweeper. Working out the possibilities on one square at a time coming at it from every different direction. If we had to think about each and every square, we would miss a lot of dinners. We have to use patterns. On the screen above, no doubt, now, your mind is shouting out, "Look at all the openings! Your mind is getting faster. Well done!

I am going to stop here now. The next Tricky Ones are very confusing to a student. To understand them, you must practice. With the above information, the average student can beat the time of 200 seconds on Minesweeper Advanced. If you have a more acute mind, a time of 150 seconds is very possible. If you can go faster than that, it is time to start thinking about buying umbrellas and rain coats. It rains a lot up in Washington State!

I have no doubt that, you the reader, will be able to develop other Tricky Ones. Minesweeper is full of them. The moment of discovery is a delicious one. Much like the moment of victory, they are times to live for. But don't forget, sometimes playing a game is just an enjoyment in its self. We are the otters of the primates. We were built to have fun! (Before all the people in red states start writing me letters, it is fun to be good. It is fun to help others. Those 3 letter words are really confusing, aren't they?)

Other Ways To Play

We live in a very competitive world. There is no denying it. But just because they set up the world like this, doesn't mean that we have to join in their game. We don't have to play Minesweeper as speed demons, sweat pouring down our brows, developing ulcers before we are 30. True, to compete seems to be at the core of most humans, but how about the rest of us?

Playing Minesweeper at a slower pace is very calming. Taking time to examine each move, looking for an opening and finally clicking, is an interesting way to play. It is an effort towards perfection. Instead of striving for the best times, try to get as many back to back wins as you can, try to better your win percentage.

Playing this way, or as a variation of play, assists in obtaining better times. It is more of a study of the game while playing fast is more of a test of your skills. In kung fu movies, the students always practice their blows in slow motion, striving for perfection in their motions. We can do this too.

I would love to tell you that Microsoft is interested in people who obtain 100 consecutive wins but first, it would be a lie, and second, I really don't think it is possible. Maybe if you were very, VERY, psychic.

Guessing

All to often, a player works through an entire screen gets close to the end without making a mistake only to find two equally valid squares, cloaked, and only one can be a mine. There is no logical way to pick one or the other. There is nothing to do but guess.

Guessing has a terrible press agent. Guessing has become a bad word these days of competition and dire consequences to failure. But it doesn't have to be.

Not all guessers are born alike. Some succeed far more than others. Realizing that, Microsoft installed an algorithm into Minesweeper to neutralize a good guessers abilities.

All too often in Minesweeper, I have to make a guess. I sweat over it. I try to apply all the logic I possess to determine which is the right way to choose. And fail almost all the time. Why?

Microsoft has slanted the situation to favor the lack of logic in guessing situations. Whether this is pure capriciousness on their part or a nod to the too often illogic of life is beyond the ken of this writer. However, don't choose randomly. Choose logically and then pick the opposite!

I have the upmost respect for some of the geniuses at Microsoft but acknowledge that given some of the weird and illogical methods chosen in some of the versions of Vista, there are evil genii alive and well hidden on the bottom floor up in Redmond. I hope they are caught soon!

Conclusion

Minesweeper is a great game and more. I think of it as mental stretching. Like athletes preparing for a run, we should stretch before using our minds at their utmost capacity. Minesweeper can do that for us.

When going into a meeting with your fellow employees who are desperately sipping their coffee, vainly trying to wake up, you are prepared. Your mind is at its peak. It is ready to race at its highest rate. Prepared by Minesweeper to anticipate the next move, you are ready for every office political move your fellow employees might try.

Who is your boss going to favor? Your temporarily slug like fellow employees or you, alive, alert, competent. To paraphrase Captain Jack Sparrow,

"The problem doesn't bother me, it is your attitude towards the problem that is the problem."

The boss is ready. He has been thinking all morning about how he is going to order his troops around, organize his army. He is at the meeting giving orders and facing a sea of blank faces. Except yours. Guess who is going to get the next raise? Thanks to Minesweeper!

Afterward

The lowest price this book can sell for on Kindle is $2.99. Why? What is wrong with $0.99? But it is their ball and their game so they get to make up the rules.

I like Kindle as their reader seems to be quite water resistant, an important concern for us deep water sailors. So, I am offering my book, just and only on Kindle for the time being. If you don't want to buy one of their machines, it is easy to down load this book onto your desktop.

At any rate, if this book creates enough interest, I will write a sequel. A book just on Tricky Ones. Hey, if those Hollywood dudes do it, why can't I?

At any rate, you are well on your way. In no time you will be receiving a letter from Microsoft! (OK, Sorry! An alleged letter!)

Good luck and good gaming. When you become a millionaire, (they pay well at Microsoft!) remember me come Christmas!

www.ingramcontent.com/pod-product-compliance
Lightning Source LLC
Chambersburg PA
CBHW051259170526
45165CB00004B/1770